I0408758

Raising Our Young:
A Story of a Bluebird Couple
Bluey and Rosey

By Virginia Cabibil Carlson

About the Author

Virginia Cabibil Carlson is a Filipina - American who lives in Minnetonka, Minnesota. She is an elementary school teacher and a nurse by profession. She is an avid bird-lover and enjoys spending time observing and taking pictures of birds in her backyard. The inspiration for this book was her grandson Laken. She is thrilled that Laken's first word in Filipino was "langgam" which means "bird" in Cebuano, her native tongue.

In memory of PA and MA and to my Family with Love

All rights reserved. No part of this book may be reproduced or transmitted in any form or by any means, electronic, mechanical, including photocopying, recording, or by any information storage and retrieval system without permission from the copyrighted owner.

Copyright © 2013 by Virginia Cabibil Carlson

ISBN-13: 978-1508601685
ISBN-10: 1508601682

I am Bluey, a bluebird. Every spring, my mate Rosey and I stay at Carlson's yard. Their place is awesome.

The spring and summer of 2012 were extra special. The Carlson's initiated a **Bird Housing Initiative Program** also known as **BHIP.** There were many styles of houses to choose from such as barn style, cabin, pagoda, beach house, church, cottage, ice fishing house, and teepee to name a few.

I showed Rosey the barn style house that was roomy and colorful. Rosey did not like this style.

2

I also found a cottage style house attached to a garden post. It had a metal roof. Rosey did not like the metal roof because it is too hot in the summer.

Rosey was really picky when it came to house hunting. She wanted the best for her babies. I love her for that!

Then, I found these two traditional, neutral toned houses attached to arbor posts. Rosey thought these styles were better. We also liked the placement of these houses so we decided to build our nest in one.

We started nest construction on May 2, 2012. I started building a nest in the house at the left of the arbor but Rosey liked the one at the right better.

Then Rosey got busy carrying materials.

I stayed nearby as Rosey foraged for materials and built the nest. We kept in touch with calls. I guarded the area for her safety. I watched her fly in and out of the house. I also stayed near to prevent her from mating with other males.

All the time, I kept watch. I perched on nearby trees, on the perching rope and on the roof of our house.

The nest was done on May 7th, 2012. The first egg was laid on May 8th. By May 12th, Rosey had laid five beautiful blue eggs.

Then Rosey sat on the eggs. During this time, Rosey developed a bare brood patch on her chest where exposed blood vessels kept the temperature warm for the eggs. Rosey attended to the eggs constantly. She only left the nest to preen and feed. I continued to keep watch.

I sang when there were no predators nearby so that she could safely leave the nest. While Rosey was out of the nest, I remained close by or inside the nest. During the night, I usually sat next to Rosey.

During this time of our relationship I gave Rosey gifts everyday - wiggly worms.

Many times, Rosey and I dined together on the arbor's roof just above the nest.

5/27/2012

Finally, the eggs cracked and baby chicks emerged. Rosey ate the eggshells. Rosey and I were happy. The following pictures were taken as dated:

6/3/2012

On June 4, 2012 at around noon, something happened to Rosey. She was not inside the nest. She did not come for treats. I looked around. Rosey was gone.

Evening came and there was no more Rosey.

I missed Rosey but I needed to be a strong father. I made sure the babies had enough food so they would grow and be strong. I hunted for insects. I also cleaned by picking up poop sacs and dropping them far from the nest so predators would not notice that there were babies inside.

Hunt and feed!

Hunt and Feed!

Hunt and Feed!

Hunt and Feed!

Hunt and Feed!

It also helped that everyday the birdfeeders were full of treats. They were the best treats - the wiggly meal-worms! Every worm–eating bird gathered to feed.

Thanks to the wiggly worms in the feeders, I was able to feed my babies all day. The babies continued to grow stronger. Dated pictures of their progress below:

6/6/2012

6/7/2012

6/8/2012

6/9/2012

They grew bigger and bigger and the nest was getting crowded. They also started growing blue feathers. Their eyes opened and were alert to their surroundings.

The babies were curious about the outside. They kept on peaking out the entryway to see the outside.

The babies continued to grow and became more curious. They were restless. They wondered about the outside and kept on peaking out the entryway.

I thought they were old enough to come out of the nest. Instead of handing them food, I just sang outside encouraging the babies to come out.

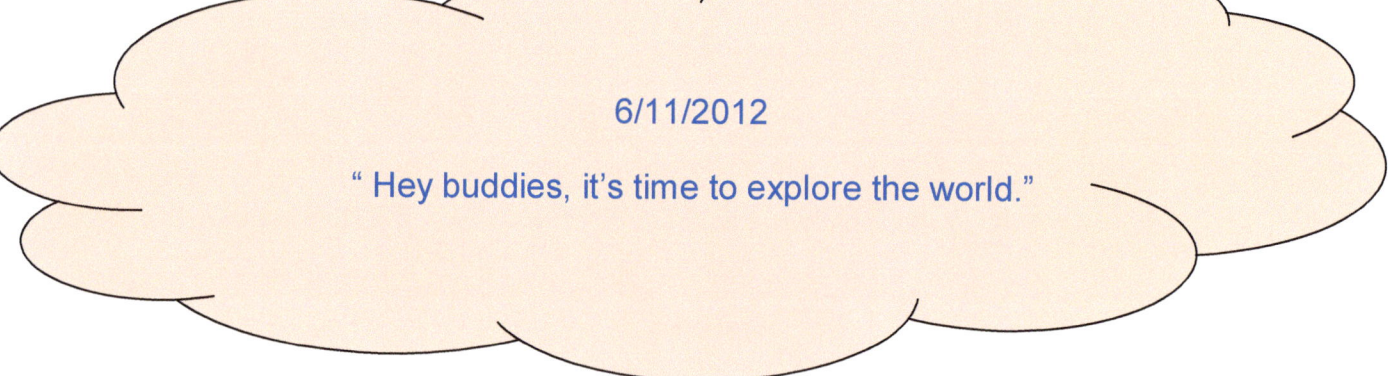

6/11/2012

" Hey buddies, it's time to explore the world."

The morning of June 12, 2012, four babies were brave enough to jump out of the nest. I watched them fly up and perch on nearby trees.

The smallest one was too scared to jump out. I continued to stay near the nest. I sang constantly, calling and luring the smallest baby to come out. I patiently encouraged the last baby to leave the nest.

Finally the baby hopped out on the ground outside while I watched for her safety from the arbor's roof, from the trees and from the perching rope. I encouraged the baby to get off the ground especially because there were cats in the area. I continuously and patiently coaxed until the baby joined the other siblings who were perching in the trees.

I was proud of my babies. If Rosey was alive she would be proud of them too. She would also be proud of me for caring for our babies so they can grow up to be lovely creatures!

I showed the babies the feeders with the best food.

We toured the different pools and other water features on the property like the waterfall, the pond, the bubble rocks, the stream, fountains and birdbaths.

I told the babies they could join the other birds for water activities. I encouraged and watched them as they observed the other birds have fun in the water.

They saw American Goldfinches, Juvenile Northern Cardinals and House Finches on the bubble rock and in the birdbaths.

They saw birds of different colors like the juvenile Audubon Warblers and juvenile Yellow Rumped Warblers enjoying the water.

They saw Tennessee Warblers and Nashville Warblers on the bubble rock.

They saw Chipping Sparrows, Goldfinches, Common Yellowthroats, Black Capped Chickadees and many birds of different colors having fun with water.

They saw Northern Cardinals enjoying a splash on a hot day. They saw Veeries stopping over to cool off in the bird pond. It was nice to hear their beautiful song.

They saw American Robins cooling off in the waterfall. They saw a baby Baltimore Oriole feeling safe to bathe by herself.

They observed Gray Catbirds and Yellow Warblers having fun together.

They saw Black Capped Chickadees hopping up and down the narrow stream.

They saw Ruby-Crowned Kinglets on the bubble rock. They also saw Brown Headed Cowbirds and Gray Catbirds soaking themselves in the pond

They saw American Tree Sparrows and Lincoln Sparrows.

They saw Rose Breasted Grosbeaks and Cedar Waxwings.

They saw Gray-Cheeked Thrushes, Chipping Sparrows and American Goldfinches.

The babies continued to explore and enjoy the surrounding neighborhood. They figured out where to find good food.

The babies discovered many places to have fun and they met birds of many different colors. They felt the place was a haven for birds.

It did not take long for my babies to join with other birds and enjoy the water. It was fun to watch them enjoying themselves. Wonderful!

They grew up to be lovely creatures. They were happy and playful babies. They sang and chased each other and flew from branch to branch in the trees. They were a delight to all who watched. I knew the fun they gave the neighborhood was priceless.

The babies continued enjoying themselves. They sang, bathed and explored the surroundings. But then the days started getting shorter and colder. It was time to go back to a place where the air was warmer.

Acknowledgment

Thanks to my husband Paul, my daughter Caroline, my friends Ely Gulani and Fr Vincent Busch for editing this book. Fr Vincent Busch is a Columban missionary in the Philippines who has authored children's books on ecology and creation.

Thanks also to my son, Chris, who assisted me in many ways with projects that helped attract birds to our yard. With his support and help, I have attracted at least seventy species of birds to our yard, some of which are pictured in this book.

www.ingramcontent.com/pod-product-compliance
Lightning Source LLC
Chambersburg PA
CBHW041510280526
45792CB00004B/1204

* 9 7 8 1 5 0 8 6 0 1 6 8 5 *